Yes, You Can Find Arrowheads

Bill Coleman

Copyright © 2016, by Bill Coleman.
All rights reserved. This book or any portion thereof may not be reproduced or used in any manner whatsoever without the express written permission of the publisher except for the use of brief quotations in a book review.

First Printing, 2013.

Contents

1	Yes, You Can Find Arrowheads	1
2	The Best Hunting Is Near Water	4
3	Hunt the Old Indian Trails	8
4	Prime Areas for Hunting	10
5	Hunted-Out Property	15
6	The Biggest Mistake That Beginners Make	17
7	Take Home Everything	20
8	Time to Get Started!	24

Yes, You Can Find Arrowheads

After reading this book, I am confident that you will have the knowledge to find arrowheads and other Indian artifacts. The only thing that will keep you from finding them will be not enough time devoted to the quest.

It's easy to find arrowheads. Many Indian artifact hunters would like for you to believe that it is as complicated as quantum physics. More often than not, the first advice from a seasoned hunter will be "go to the library and begin researching."

I believe that the more you know about the artifacts that you find and the people who once owned them, the more meaning they will have for you, but most people have a desire to begin finding artifacts as soon as possible. Most people work hard for most of the week, and they need a little fun during their leisure time. Almost everybody that I know would get a bigger rush from finding an arrowhead than they would from a trip to the library.

I have read every local history book that I could find that might possibly help me know the prehistoric people who once lived in my area. I became obsessed with gaining more knowledge. I put in so much time at the library, local museums, the Internet and in the woods looking for artifacts that I decided to write a local history book of my own.

You can find my book, *The History of Rock Mountain in Jefferson County, Alabama*, online at Amazon and Barnes and Noble. (You can download it as an eBook at Amazon for only $ 3.99.) In that book, I cover Prehistoric Native Americans and their artifacts in more detail than I will in this one. I want to keep this book as simple as possible for those who just want to get out there and start hunting. I have little doubt that when those who finish this book get into the woods, creeks, and fields and begin finding artifacts, they will want to find websites and other books to learn more about their finds.

Just believing that you will find artifacts is the main thing that's going to make it probable that you will find them. Once I made up my mind that I was going to begin finding them, I did. The more I found, the more I found.

Nobody knows with certainty even an approximate number, but when Columbus "discovered" America in 1492, it was heavily populated. Native Americans had been living on the continent for 12,000+ years. During that time, millions of Native Americans used tools that were manufactured from stone. Doesn't it make sense that there are artifacts near you that are just waiting to be picked up, and though you may have never found a single artifact, you've probably stepped on them, possibly on your own property? The last part of that statement isn't the least bit far-fetched. People often find Prehistoric Native American artifacts in their yards when they are tilling ground for a new garden or when they are putting in a pool.

Many people believe that hunting arrowheads is backbreaking, meticulous, work. It can be, but the remedy for that is don't dig. Once you become very good at finding artifacts, there will be more than enough on the surface, and your eyes will be drawn to them. You just have find enough places to hunt.

Hunting arrowheads can be relaxing. You can set your own pace and take a break when you feel like it. For me, there is nothing more relaxing that sitting on a creek bank after a couple of hours of arrowhead hunting. If you are searching for a healthy outdoor activity this is it. What other pastime will give you exercise, teach you history, and provide you with free souvenirs to take home?

It's a good idea to be cautious about walking on someone else's property without permission. I only hunt arrowheads within walking distance of my home. I know the area and I feel comfortable where I hunt. I wouldn't just park my car anywhere and start searching. That might get my car towed or me arrested. The world did not used to be that way, but

it is now. People are much more possessive of their property than they once were, and they are more suspicious of strangers. That said, if you ask politely there's a very good chance that you will get permission. In fact, some people will even be encouraging and helpful when you ask.

Most people are visually attracted to arrowheads, and for most people, that is the Prehistoric Indian artifact that they favor over most others. But just because it has a point, doesn't mean it's necessarily an arrowhead. Most of what is commonly thought to be arrowheads, aren't. Most are knives and scrapers. Some are spear and dart points. If the artifact has a point, many knowledgeable artifact hunters simply call them "points."

In this book, I will use arrowhead and artifact interchangeably.

The Best Hunting Is Near Water

If you hunt long enough, you will find artifacts everywhere imaginable. Any disturbed area could turn up artifacts. Man or nature, or a combination of both, are responsible for disturbed ground. Examples of man-made disturbed ground are construction sites, plowed fields, and clear-cut lumber harvesting. Wind and rain are natural events that could disturb the ground. Some of your best hunting days will be a result of a combination of man-made and natural, for example, a recently plowed field after a heavy rain.

If you want to narrow your hunting down to where arrowheads are most likely to be, find water that has been in the same place for many centuries- natural creeks, rivers, lakes, and other bodies of water. Prehistoric Indians lived on those creeks and rivers off and on for thousands of years. At times, the creek and river banks were lined with Indian dwellings. Villages covered acres of land, and sometimes they were built on even the smallest streams. At various times throughout history, it rained much more than it is does now, and some of those smaller, seasonal streams that we have today would have held much more water.

Narrow the places that you most frequently hunt to disturbed ground near water, and it becomes almost certain that with enough searching, you will find arrowheads.

There were millions of Prehistoric Indians in North America over the course of 12,000+ years, and they lived near water. Remember that the next time that you see an old creek or river. Shut your eyes, and imagine Indian camps and villages lining the banks. There isn't an old creek or river in North America that didn't have Indian camps and villages on its banks.

Hunt the high areas where they lived and the low areas, even flood plains, where they might have farmed and hunted. Flood plains at the bend of a creek or river can be especially good places to hunt if the cause of the bend is water rushing against a hill or mountainside. Flood waters often wash artifacts from the creek or river. When the water recedes, they are left on land. I have found hundreds of artifacts at one of those spots.

An area like the one in the above picture can have artifacts at the flood plain, in the water, or at the top of the hill where they lived. It's not difficult to conclude that a creek like this one would have flowed in the same place for thousands of years because the water couldn't have been anywhere else during normal flow. That makes it a lot easier to know where the artifacts are likely to be.

Some hunters are very good at finding artifacts actually in the water. Often, there are more artifacts in the water than on the banks for two reasons: (1) They have washed down from upstream and from higher ground and (2) They have eroded from the water banks over time as rushing water cut into the banks. Flowing water will eventually push artifacts against bends in the creek or river, trap them in and under debris, push them into bigger bodies of water, or even push them back up on land again until another big rain event pushes them back into the water. Arrowheads and other artifacts near moving water, move with water. They can end up in a lot of places that are hard to imagine. I have found water-stained arrowheads on higher ground than any flood that we can imagine would have put them there.

Hunting in the water is a special skill, and some people become very good at it– so good that they rarely venture out of the water in their search for artifacts. Unless they are in very shallow water and freshly washed there from land, it's harder for a novice to find artifacts in the water, but once a hunter gets good at it, he often finds more than his fair share of arrowheads because he doesn't have to look as many places as hunters who hunt dry land. Certainly, always scan the water's edge for newly deposited artifacts, like the one in the picture below. They are often easy to spot because they are clean and haven't been water-stained.

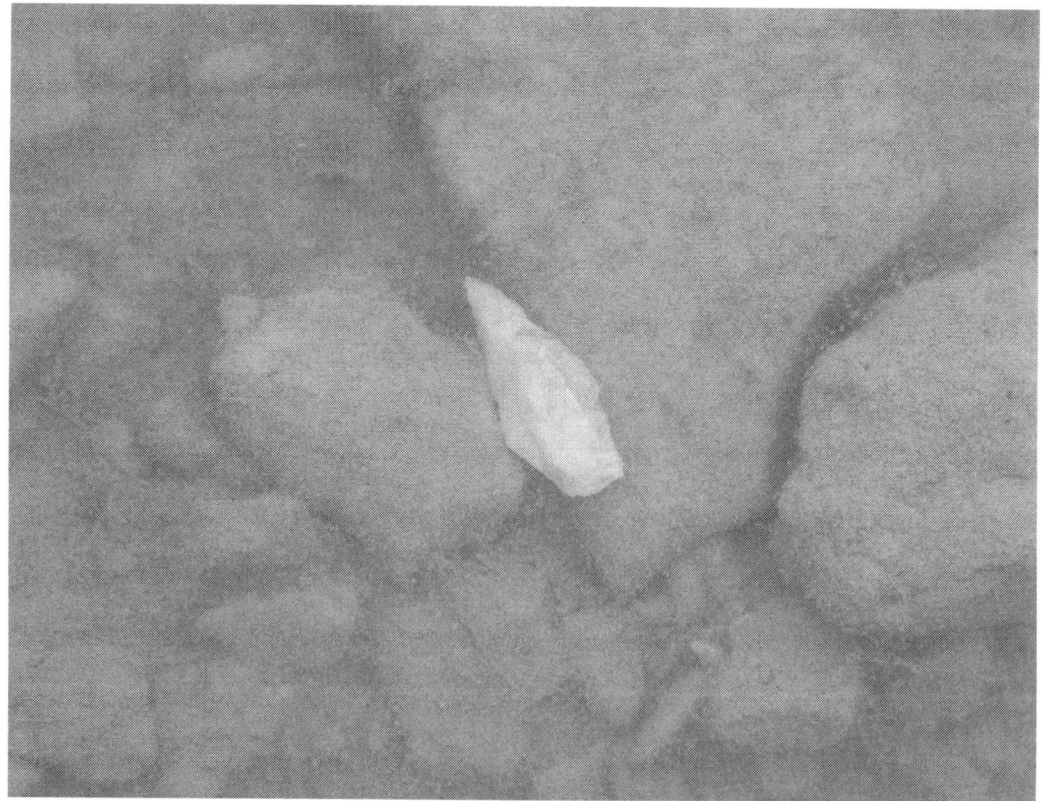

I suggest you stay out of the water until you master finding them on dry land. One exception to that is the land area between the bank and the water, after a good rain. A good rain will cause rushing water to cut into this area, and, more often than not, the rain event will not push the artifact completely into the water. Part of it will be exposed. Once you gain experience at finding artifacts, that partially exposed artifact will stick out like a sore thumb because it will be clean and look much different than the surrounding area.

This is what most people would never notice, but what you will after you finish this book and put some time into training your eye:

Hunt the Old Indian Trails

Trails and old dirt roads that "make sense" geographically to be where they are at are good places to hunt for artifacts. If a trail or road makes sense geographically today, it made sense thousands of years ago for the same reasons. In my area there is an old dirt road that runs across the top of Rock Mountain that has drop-offs on both sides– one side is a bluff and the other side is a steep mountain. It makes perfect sense for a road to be on top of that mountain now, and it always did in the past. It's safe to call a road like than "an Old Indian Trail."

When I walk down that road, I think about all of the people that have walked it before me, going back more than 10,000 years. It's impossible to estimate how many tools and arrowheads on that road were lost or thrown away because they were broken or used to the point that it made more sense to just manufacture another one. But if the number was known, it would be staggering. When you are walking down an old road like this, keep your eyes on the ground because there are artifacts nearby.

It wouldn't hurt to ask people that you know, whose roots go back in your area many years, if they know of any old Indian trails, but you are not likely to leave the conversation any more enlightened than you were to begin with. Most people make assumptions than aren't valid and stories often become embellished with time.

Maps with Indian trail routes are sometimes available, but it's easier to just find them yourself. Again, unless the area that you want to hunt has been affected by modern construction and development, just imagine the route that you would want to take from one place to another and search there. Put in enough time and you will find artifacts. If you find artifacts or even just lithic debris, search every piece of disturbed ground, and continue revisiting the area after every good rain or after the ground has been disturbed by other means.

If you find a trail and follow it to water, you have probably found an area that's prime for arrowhead hunting.

Prime Areas for Hunting

At one point near that old road across the crest of Rock Mountain there is a pass through the mountain. It's a place where I cross from one side of the mountain to the other, and it would be a place where others had done that same thing for more than 10,000 years. Even better for artifact hunting, a pretty creek flows through the pass. How could there not be artifacts in a place like this? I have found hundreds of nice artifacts near this spot. In fact, I have found enough artifacts to know that at various times in history, Prehistoric Indian villages would have covered two continuous miles of this area.

Why would an area like that (partially pictured above and below) be attractive to Prehistoric Native Americans? (1) The creek provided a water source, (2) the bottom of the bluffs provided shelter, (3) the top of the bluffs provided a place to survey the area for game and maybe even enemies, (4) the road across the top served as an Indian trail.

When you find an area like that one, hit it hard and keep coming back after rains. Why after rains? It's really obvious once you think about it. Rains wash artifacts out of the ground. The more erosion, the sooner artifacts will wash from the ground. If the ground is partially bare of vegetation they can be beaten out of the ground over time, even if the ground is flat.

The area that I just described is prime for hunting arrowheads. Most places aren't prime, but prime hunting spots are not rare. Areas similar to the one pictured are common in much of the Southeastern United States. Other parts of the country have their own prime areas, though they may not look even remotely similar to the pictures.

Broaden your thinking about where you can find arrowheads. Even if the ground is mostly wooded, there will still be places to look. Search ditches. Search mounds of dirt that were piled during construction or road building.

Search areas around power lines, especially where dirt has been removed to plant the poles. Get the idea? Any place where the ground has been disturbed is a place to look.

In the picture below, look at the trails on the power line. That's where you should look, especially if there is old water nearby. Artifacts most often originate on high ground, but they are often found on the hillsides and at the bottom because they are moved there by weather events.

Where are other not-so-prime areas that can still be productive? Here are a few places they could be, and after you read them I'm certain that you will think of some lost opportunities (I know I do): logging trails and clear-cuts, road construction, home construction, pond construction, and shopping center development. That's just a few to get your mind moving in the right direction. If any of those places in your area is near a creek or river, count on artifacts being there.

Agricultural fields can be prime, even those that wouldn't be if you were just confined to hunting the surface. The area has basically been excavated for you, and it may be a place that will produce over and over because the ground might possibly be turned over each planting season. A good rain soon after plowing will make things even better for you. Just as some hunters only hunt creeks, others only hunt fields, often because they are convinced that the only good hunting is in fields.

After a good rain has hit a freshly plowed field, arrowheads are often completely exposed on the surface, but sometimes, just like anywhere else, only part of the arrowhead will be exposed. That's when knowing how to spot the material that was used to manufacture the artifacts is beneficial. Would you have known this might have been a complete arrowhead?

Since we don't have much agriculture in this area, I will search anywhere and everywhere. Hunting a wide variety of places opens your mind to more possibilities. Though I would never miss an opportunity to hunt a plowed field, I wouldn't want to restrict myself to that. I like the challenge of finding undiscovered sites and the beautiful scenery that is most often absent from fields.

Notice that I have mentioned "your area" several times already. That was purposeful. The materials used to make artifacts vary from place to place. The more you know about the materials native to where you are hunting, the easier it will be to find arrowheads and other artifacts, at least in the beginning.

Hunted-Out Property

When inquiring about hunting opportunities, you will probably hear: "Don't waste your time, that's been hunted-out." The fact that artifacts move with water flow and soil disruption means that an area can never be totally hunted-out. An area can be hunted to the point that it becomes harder than it once was to find them, but it can never be totally cleaned out. This is one of the most prevalent fallacies regarding hunting Indian artifacts. It is true that the casual hunter might have a tough time ever finding arrowheads on so-called "hunted-out" land, but when you get very good at finding them, you will be able to accomplish what most can't.

Many who will read this book live in densely populated areas. Conventional wisdom leads most to believe that arrowheads are way out in the woods or in the "country." They are everywhere. I live in a rural suburban area. I find them way out in the woods and within sight of homes. I have found several within sight of the home where I live now. I have found them in drainage ditches. I have found them on dirt roads when they were "beat out" of the ground by hard rains. The next picture shows an arrowhead that my wife found in the middle of a dirt road. Notice how it blends in with its surroundings.

People are stepping on arrowheads close to where you live, but they rarely see them because they haven't trained their eyes. When yours become trained, you will find them in areas where others don't bother to look. Your eyes will be continuously scanning the ground while walking, even when you aren't arrowhead hunting.

I have to hide my smile when I'm told that there are no arrowheads near my home. I have hundreds on my walls and in boxes that prove otherwise. Most of the time, I'll just let the people who tell me that there are no arrowheads here continue believing what is not fact because there will be less people looking for them.

Put in your time and keep your eyes on the ground and you will be surprised where you will find arrowheads.

Never believe that all of the arrowheads have been found anywhere they've been found before, and never assume that they aren't where you haven't looked.

The Biggest Mistake That Beginners Make

Now I'm going to tell you the biggest mistake that most beginners make: They look for arrowheads. If that's you, try it again, but cease making that mistake. Get back to the woods, creeks, and fields to train your eye. Then get ready to spend some money on some arrowhead frames.

So if you aren't looking for arrowheads, then what? Imagine a house being built on site. What do the workers have to continually clean up or else they are buried in it? Answer: Waste material and leftovers like wood and roofing scraps, saw dust, bent nails, broken bricks, chunks of mortar, and pieces of insulation. The same has been true throughout the history of construction and manufacturing.

In the above picture, notice how different the white and gray rock looks from the surrounding rock. The more of this in the area, the better the site. The more of this that you find, the better you will get at spotting it. It really is the key to finding Prehistoric Indian sites. It's impossible to overstate that.

For every tool or arrowhead that Prehistoric Native Americans produced, there was many, many times more pieces of waste material produced—sometimes more than one hundred times as much. This waste material is called *lithic debris*. It's much easier to find lithic debris than it is to find finished arrowheads and tools. Types of lithic debris are flakes, chips, and cobble. (Cobble is the base material that they worked with.) Waste flakes were sometimes quickly worked into simple tools, but more often they, along with the rest of lithic debris, were just left where they fell.

Here is some lithic debris that I quickly gathered in an area where I have found many finished artifacts:

In my area the material of choice was chert. In the midst of dirt and soft, dull colored rock like shale and sandstone, it really stands out. In addition to white, chert can be many colors, including pink, black, gray, orange, yellow and even blue. After you train your eyes to spot it, you can see the tiniest of flakes and chips from quite a distance.

When you first begin bringing these rocks home, if you show them to a friend, he is likely to call them "just rocks." When you begin finding pretty arrowheads he will change his tune and might even ask you to take him hunting.

You might want to show your friend what "just a rock" looks like and what a "worked rock" looks like. The way I explain it to those who question my "rocks" is by asking them if they've seen a chert road. Then I ask them if what they are holding in their hand looks like that chert. When they inevitably tell me "no," I point out some of the flaking on the debris that is obviously not natural. Even though chert was the favored material in my area, I also find some artifacts made from jasper, quartz, and sometimes even bone. After you spend some time hunting, you will learn the materials in your area.

Don't assume that chert will necessarily be the preferred material in your area. Prehistoric Native Americans loved working with chert, but it was not available in all places. They used a wide variety of native materials and "foreign" materials through trade routes.

So, train your eye to look for waste material. When you find lithic debris in any amount, search the immediate area hard. Make sure you remember the spot and never completely cease searching it. You might want to slack up when you don't find any for a while, but always eventually get back to that spot. Rains or anything else that moves soil around will turn up more artifacts.

Take Home Everything

I bring home everything, even the smallest flakes for two reasons: (1) I hunt the same areas over and over, and I don't want to keep seeing the same waste material and (2) I believe that even waste material are artifacts, and it should be kept with the rest of the artifacts that are found. In fact, archaeologists record everything that they find on a site, which is why you will often see records of thousands of artifacts that were removed from unremarkable sites.

At the first good spot that we found after we began hunting with a purpose, we picked up a sack-full of lithic debris, a couple of broken tools, and some hammerstones. (Hammerstones are large tools used to make other, mostly smaller, tools.) We didn't get much rain for several months after that, but since it was our only spot, we kept hunting it until we had picked up every flake and chip. When we finally began to get some good rains, the arrowheads started washing up.

No doubt somebody had been hunting the area before we found it and either didn't know what hammerstones are or didn't care about them. We needed a good rain to show us that it was a good spot. We have been hunting the area for more than five years now, and whoever was hunting it before us gave up on it. After each rain, we picked up everything on the site, even the tiniest flakes. I guess they had good reason to give up. Remember this: If you want to keep finding arrowheads on a site, be the first there after each good rain.

While shape is possibly an indication of an artifact, flaking makes it certain that you have found an artifact. Once your eyes become trained, they will be drawn to shapes, flaking, and even patina.

Go hunting enough times and you will find many different types of artifacts, probably everything from large hammerstones to tiny little arrowheads, as small as 1/4" in height.

After you have been hunting a while, rocks like this will draw your eyes to them:

I have seen partially covered arrowheads too many times to even estimate, but the excitement is still always there.

Depending on your area, you might also find pottery shards (examples below) scattered on the ground. In some locations, the ground is literally covered with pottery shards. If you find a spot like this, you have found a village site. It is beyond the scope of this book, but you can roughly date a site based on whether pottery, and what type, is present. In my Rock Mountain book, I explore this in more detail.

If there is doubt in your mind regarding whether you have found an actual artifact, bring it home. When I first began searching for artifacts, I found some made from bone. I didn't know at the time what I had found. About three years later I was looking through some lithic debris that I had found from back then. Mixed in with it was some bone pieces that I had brought home because they looked unusual. The "artifact" in them jumped out almost immediately.

That's an indication of how little I knew then and how much I had learned since. Unfortunately, I left the best bone artifact in the woods. It didn't take me three years to learn what I had left. I saw a picture of a trigger awl in a book and remembered leaving the one that I had found. Bone is an organic material, so it is very susceptible to moisture and humidity, especially in the Deep South where I live. I'm very happy when I find a bone artifact because it is very uncommon here.

If it looks like it might possibly be a worked artifact, bring it home. Things will eventually fall into place, and later on you will want to go through your questionables and give them another look. If you are on a site where you've found artifacts or even a lot of lithic debris, look at everything with a discerning eye. If it looks even slightly different from the rest of the things you normally see, pick it up, imagine what it may have been have been used for, and then look for how it might have been worked into what you've imagined. Would you have known this was a metate and mano used for processing seeds, nuts, and grains?

Time to Get Started!

At the beginning of this book, I mentioned that you will not have to do a lot of research before beginning your first arrowhead hunt. I hope that after reading this book that you want to learn more about your artifacts and the people who left them for you to find. At the very least, you are going to have questions about some of your finds. The Internet is the best place to look for the answers to those questions. With enough time spent searching for it, on the Internet there's an answer for every question that you have.

You will certainly want to join some of the Internet forums. There, you can see what others have found and even post pictures of your finds. It usually doesn't take long before a veteran hunter has commented on your post. Three of the best forums are TreasureNet.com (scroll down the TreasureNet forum page to North American Indian Artifacts), Arrowheadology.com, and Arrowheads.com.

I also encourage you to visit your local history museums. There, you can get an up-close look at artifacts that were found in your area, and you will better-recognize artifacts when you come across them on your arrowhead hunts.

It makes a collection more desirable to others if all of the artifacts are from a specific locality. The collection will also be more valuable to other collectors if it ever comes up for sale (I would never sell my collection, but it is wise to think about those things because even collections like mine will belong to someone else at some point). If you do hunt different localities, keep separate the collection based on where you found them. If you frame them, and you should, write on the back of the frame where they came from. You can even use a GPS to pinpoint the location, print it out, and attach it to the back of the frame.

If you frame your arrowheads, never use glue or wire to hold your arrowheads in place. I use shadow boxes with foam inserts. (One is pictured at the beginning of this book.) The foam presses against the glass, holding the arrowheads in place. This method does no damage to artifacts, plus I can open a case and rearrange when I find better arrowheads to display. With glue or wire, the arrowheads are frozen in place, making it impossible to look at the reverse side. You can easily find foam shadow boxes on the Internet.

The last tip I'll give you: If you know an experienced arrowhead hunter, ask him to take you hunting. Your friend is probably not going to show you his best places, but even if he takes you to his worst place and you find nothing, he will show you the methodology that he uses. Have your friend to show you flakes, chips, and cobble, so that you can recognize it when you see it. Take it home and study it.

But don't fret over it if you can't find anybody to take you. You've learned enough from reading this book. Good luck!